THOUGHT CATALOG BOOKS

To All the Ones I've Ever
Loved

To All the Ones I've Ever Loved

KIANA AZIZIAN

Thought Catalog Books

Brooklyn, NY

THOUGHT CATALOG BOOKS

Copyright © 2016 by Kiana Azizian

All rights reserved. Published by Thought Catalog Books, a division of The Thought & Expression Co., Williamsburg, Brooklyn. Founded in 2010, Thought Catalog is a website and imprint dedicated to your ideas and stories. We publish fiction and non-fiction from emerging and established writers across all genres. For general information and submissions: manuscripts@thoughtcatalog.com.

First edition, 2016

ISBN 978-1945796296

10 9 8 7 6 5 4 3 2 1

Cover design by © KJ Parish

For all the ones I've ever loved—
who couldn't manage to love me in return.

For every girl out there who's ever had her heart broken.

Just know,
you are never alone.

Contents

Part II. The Heartbreakers

Part III. The Destruction

Here's to the Heartbroken

This is for the broken-hearted.
For anyone who is in a great deal of ache.
Here's to the people who feel a tightness in their chest
and a void in their hearts.
For anyone who has ever known the pain and agony of heartbreak.
This is for those who can't think, who can't eat, and who can't sleep.
Here's to loving someone who doesn't love you back.
This is for enduring one of the worst types of pains;
the cruelest type of hurt one can know.
Here's to undeservingly putting the needs of someone else
above your own.
This piece is for anyone who fights too hard
for someone who isn't worthy of their love.
To the people who care for someone who cannot handle their
passion.
For those who know how it feels to have their beating heart
ripped out of their chest,
And has held that same bleeding heart in their bare hands.
Here's to finding yourself within the midst of devastation.
Fighting like hell to stay alive,
While picking up your broken piece and gluing them back together.
This, right here, is for anyone who has found themselves
slowly turning bitter and jaded.
Who have blocked out love, in terror of getting hurt again.

Here's to being flawed, to being imperfect, and to being damaged.
Here's to being human.

But mostly, this is amending you on your accomplishments,

For not allowing any of the above to stand in your way.
This is for those who have risen above misery,
Pulled themselves from the deeps of the ocean.
These words are for those who have found the courage and strength
to love and trust again.
To conquering your fear of being alone
and putting yourself out there,
Even after countless rejections.
Here's to never allowing another to put a value on your worth.
To the people who never permit another human being
to regulate their happiness,
And who control their own emotions and feelings.
This is for anyone who has tried and failed, then tried again.
For the people will never allow evil to evade.
Cheers to the those who have found the strength to put themselves
before toxic people.
Who have found clarity in setting themselves free from the
destruction of another being.
For the people who have struggled to stay above water,
And somewhere along the way, learned to enjoy the waves of the sea.

Here is to you,
Because you didn't allow another human to drown you,
And have always succeeded to stay afloat.
But mostly this is for you, my lovely.
For you are not as damaged as you feel.
You are not as destroyed as another has force you to become.
Here's to trying to the best of your abilities.
To believing in you.
Here's to not allowing the word "broken" to define you.
To being one of the strongest people you know.
Here's to rising above pain and finding happiness once again.
To no longer being broken-hearted.
Here is to finally healing and recovering.

To not feeling shattered beyond repair.
Here's to never losing yourself to another.

Here's to loving again.
To loving yourself again.
This is all for you,
Because, my goodness,
Am I proud of you.

I am proud of you.
I am *so* proud of you.

Broken

The Sun and the Moon

The sun burned so brightly,
she hid behind the shadows,
allowing the moon to appear from the darkness.
The sun loved the moon so much,
she dimmed her radiance,
to permit his crescent to glow.
They both knew the rules of our universe
would keep them from being together,
but they didn't mind.
For their love story is the most beautiful to ever exist.
And they would spend eternity chasing one another to prove so.

2

Expectations

Are we expecting too much from love?
By placing it upon a pedestal where it doesn't belong
and worshiping the very concept of its existence?

Why are we expecting so much from one simple thing?

Magical Beginnings

I miss the young girl I use to be.

She was perfect,
unbroken
unmarked.

She was naïvely stunning,
believing this world was made of magic
while trusting it was filled with love.

4

Time

Time,
a powerful object.
Controlling our every move,
our every decision.
Ruling our entire lives.
Constantly ticking and ticking,
reminding us of what little control we actually own.

5

Boys will be Boys

When she was younger,
they said if a boy was mean
it meant he liked her.

I guess she never stopped believing he did.

Human

We're all a bit broken.
We're all a bit damaged.
We're all struggling a bit to glue back together our pieces
in hopes of creating something worth existing.

We're all a bit human, just trying to survive.

Transformation

She was like the ocean breeze
eloquently calming the souls of everyone she ever adored.

Now she's a hurricane
dismantling others with the simple flicker of her heart.

8

Fake

She was too real for our tremendous fake world.
And this is why she knew so much pain.

Ignorance

The more she looked,
the harder it became to find happiness.
Ignorance was a blissful place to reside,
for beauty was becoming more difficult to find.

Rejection

Rejection.
The worst feeling in the world.

Not being good enough.
Insufficient.
Undeserving.

Unworthy.

11

Destruction

You
don't
destroy
the
ones
you
love.

Hell of a Girl

To them, she was a hell of a girl.

Yet most days, she felt like a girl stuck in hell.

Simple Lover

She was simple in nature.
All she ever wanted was a man to love her
for everything she simply could not.

Painfully Beautiful

How is it possible something so beautiful can be in so much pain?

Hostility

She was bitter, jaded, and angry.

Honestly, she wasn't always like this.
There was a reason behind her spiteful manner.

Simply, she was in so much ache.
Fighting to stay alive in her very own personal hell.
Fighting to not drown in the ocean of her past.

Fighting to fall in love with this world,
the same world that has tried to break her.

Depression

Depression often got the best of her,
draining her of happiness,
while stripping her sorrow.

Until one day,
she accepted the controlling sadness,
depriving it of all its power.

Unspoken Words

Her words whisper lies,
while her scares scream the truth.

Beautiful Mess

Her eyes were controlled by sadness.
Her lips by dishonesty.
Her arms by disaster.
Her heart by pain.

She was a beautiful mess,
patched together by everything that tried to shatter her.

Appeal

She was an emotional being.
She felt everything too much.
Some days she hated herself for it.
Wishing she could turn off her feeling,
craving to be anybody but herself.
Wanting to be the 'cool girl.'
Wanting to be the 'chill girl.'
Wanting to be the 'it girl.'

She could not understand how they did it.

Unfortunately, she never would.

And although she didn't realize it,
she was more appealing than they ever could be.

Emptiness

She poured her heart and soul into everything she'd ever loved, causing her to permanently feel empty.

Damsel in Distress

She built herself a tower so high,
not even the most charming of princes could save her.

Fire

She couldn't find it in herself to trust again.
She'd been burned too many times before.

The fire that used to live inside now terrifies her.

Ghost

She was afraid of the dark,
not because of monsters or ghosts,
because the blackness had a disastrous way of shouting the truth.

Strength

She slowly began to drown,
always trying to keep the others afloat.

Old Habits

Old habits die hard,
and they're slowly starting to kill me.

26

Broken Masterpiece

Broken: a contrary word by definition.

There is sadness in the loss of everything shattered by its destruction,
tearing down all that use to be.

There is faith in the reconstruction of all the pieces,
building up into a greater being.

She was broken;
a perfectly fragmented masterpiece.

27

Desires

She always wants what she can't have.
This was no coincidence.

She found an appeal in taking things that weren't meant for her.

A pride in mugging things of their loveliness,
just as the world once did to her.

28

Doubts

She began to question love, the one thing she always wanted.
The one thing she always believed in.
The one thing that had always been there for her.

Beautiful Things

Why do people always find the need
to be devoid beautiful things?

Space

We all exist under the same moon,
allowing gravity to hold us down,
unconsciously moving with the rotation of the earth.

We're all just stuck on different levels of the same game.

Forever & Always

She carries around the ones who left
in the deepest pockets of her heart.
For this is the only way she can still believe in the term "always."

Fatal Flaw

She was too much and that was her fatal flaw.

She cared too much,
about all the right things and all the wrong people.
She gave too much,
slowly causing herself to fade away.
She loved too much,
for those who didn't deserve an ounce of her affection.

She gave too much and tried too hard for people who cared too little.

She was the most beautiful girl alive,
struggling to see it for herself.

Too Beautiful for Words

Thank the ones who broke you,
for they are usually too beautiful to describe with words.

Soulmates

Every so often,
we will come across a soul made for our own.

These people rarely stay around for too long.

For if they did,
the undeniable power of their love would completely ruin us.

Conditional Love

She lived her life through the opinions of people
who never noticed how striking she was.
She existed through the eyes of those who couldn't see her value.

She allowed her demons to determine her self-worth,
loathing herself for it all.

36

Longing

How is it possible to miss someone you've never even met?

Collisions

The universe tilted and turned,
changing its predetermined direction,
shifting itself off course.

All in the hopes one day,
his and her paths would collide.

If I Let You In

If I let you in,
promise not to break anything like the others,
promise not to leave like them as well.

Promise to love me like they couldn't achieve.

Part 2

The Heartbreakers

M.E.K.

He was my first love,
starting all this insanity.
He was brilliant.
He was kind.
He was humorous.

He set the bar high,
hindering every man who ever followed.

S.P.M.

He was poised in his entire being,
strikingly stunning.
His confidence was inspiring.

He was the first person to ever make me feel beautiful,
something I will never be able to repay him for.

G.J.R.

His thirst for the world was moving.
His kindness was hidden behind a layer of cockiness.

He was the most irritating—yet charming—person I've ever known.

If fate had allowed,
I would have spent the rest of my days drinking his essence,
while tasting his lips.

I.D.L.

I never knew the true love of a man until him.
He was sweet and gentle.
His arms felt like home.

I could see his love was real in the way he looked at me
as if I was the prettiest girl in his world.

He was everything I never knew I needed.

A.M.N.

He was perfection.
He was all.

He is still everything my heart has ever desired,
and I will spend the rest of my days waiting to meet him again.

T.L.K.

Youthful was the best way to describe him.
His energy was contagious, taking over my entire body.

His love was healing,
reassuring me there was still good left in this world.

45

D.S.A.

He was the devil, yet he dressed like you and me.
He was determined,
selfishly taking whatever he wanted.

He was everything I despised in a man.
Still to this day, I couldn't tell you why I even cared.

His mark will forever be left on my skin,
reciting a story I've ever had the courage to tell.

The Destruction

What If?

Maybe in another world, there could be a "you" and "me."
An "us."
Maybe on another planet,
or maybe in an alternative realm,
"we" could exist.

Maybe,
just maybe,
in another life,
our love could succeed.

Please Don't Go

Why does it seem like the one who promised to never leave
are the first to go?
And the ones who promised to not hurt us
do the most?

Nonexistent

She was drunk off the idea of him,
falling for a person who never existed.
He was nothing but a pigment of her wild imagination,
created by all her dreams and ambitions.

He wasn't real,
at least not that version of him.
He only existed upon her will.

She was in love with a man who this world never knew.

He was everything she'd ever wanted,
perfectly calculated through the faults of the previous.

His false essence left her hung over at the very thought of him.

(S.P.M.)

49

Imperfections

These days,
I'm not even sure who you are.

But the man I knew was like the ocean,
the moon,
the stars,
all the galaxies,
collided into one.

He was impeccably perfect for my flawed heart.

(I.D.L.)

Senses

I see you among strangers in the streets.
I smell you in drops of rain.
I feel you between the blades of grass.
I hear you through the waves of the ocean.
I taste you in the air in which I breathe.

My entire world is made up of you.

(A.M.N.)

51

Shots

He smiled,
as he tilted his head back and took a shot of me.

(S.P.M.)

52

What Took You So Long?

"What took you so long?" he gently whispered in my ear.

I couldn't help but smile.
I'd been wondering the same thing.

(G.J.R.)

53

Summer Days

Please, one more time.

Tell me that story.

The one with the young boy and girl,
sitting under that giant oak tree.
Summer breeze running through their hair,
while time seemed to stand still.

Tell me how they loved one another so much,
they couldn't find the words to convey.

So they sat quietly under that tree,
thinking about life.

Dreaming of one together.

(M.E.K.)

Glances

He was the most beautiful creature she'd laid eyes upon,
chiseled to perfection.
Perfectly sculpted.
He stole her breath away with just once glance.
Shaking up her entire world
solely with the force of his bewitching eyes.

(S.P.M.)

First Kiss

I still remember the first moment our lips touched.

I'd never tasted anything so gorgeous.

Our mouths like magnetic forces,
captivating us together.

(G.J.R.)

Mysteries

She had met him by chance.
Still to this day she wasn't sure why he had been brought into her life.

His purpose remained a mystery,
which was her favorite thing about him.

(T.L.K.)

Mixed Signals

He is a being full of mixed signals,
feeding her hungry,
overthinking soul.

(D.S.A.)

Slumber

As I sleep,
your name outlines my lips,
your love encloses my heart.

(A.M.N.)

59

Dancing

He smelled like sex,
erotically filling her nostrils,
exciting her with the thought of his body,
pressed against hers.

Dancing,
together,
as one.

(T.L.K.)

Beyond Words

No combination of arbitrary letters could capture him.
He was indescribable.

He was simply beyond words.

(A.M.N.)

Unravel

In one night he unraveled the wrongs of all the men who preceded.
With a simple kiss on the forehead,
he helped undress the walls protecting her fragile heart.

(T.L.K.)

62

Infidelity

Even though he's with her,
he still has eyes for me.

And I can't help but like the way they look at me.

(D.S.A.)

Dreams

I hope one morning you wake up
and realize I was the answer to all your wildest dreams.

(I.D.L.)

Attraction

I'd never know electricity until your touch,
lust until your embrace,
passion until your kiss,

love until your soul.

(G.J.R.)

Crowds

And when all my dreams come true,
I'll look for you between the crowds.

(A.M.N.)

Blink of an Eye

Her world shifted in a second,
an instant of pure bliss,
when his eyes met hers for the first time.
In that moment,
she didn't realize she would never be the same.

Her entire life had shifted with the blink of an eye.

(S.P.M.)

Come Back

Don't you dare ask me to come back now.

As if silence didn't consume us, tearing us apart from the inside out.
As if you didn't set me on fire, slowly burning me to the ground.
As if we're still those people who weren't destroyed
through the destruction of all this madness.

Please don't come crawling in return to me now.
Because
maybe,
just maybe,
I might consider taking you back.

(I.D.L.)

Memories

I hope my memory haunts you,
because yours still visits me all the time.

(S.P.M.)

Spotless Disaster

She was a disaster waiting to happen.
He was the calm before the storm.

Together, they were faultless.

Flawlessly forming into one spotless hurricane,
demolishing everything standing in their way.

(G.J.R.)

70

Secrets

You are my favorite secret.
I am at loss for words
because of you.

(T.L.K.)

Flights

And as he boarded that last plane,
tears validated all the words I never succeeded to say.

(A.M.N.)

72

Chance

He was mystical.
He was enchanting.
He was unattainable.

She would have given anything for a chance to love him again.

(A.M.N.)

Alterations

You changed me,
morphed me into the person
who I never had the courage to become on my own,
inspired me to become the best version of myself.
You motivated me
to become a person who you could fall in love with.

Hoping one day that you would be able to return my love for you.

(G.J.R.)

74

Searching

Your love broke me.
Allowing myself to recreate the most beautiful version of me.
Without the destructive power of your love,
I would still be that innocent,
naïve girl who was searching for something.

She was searching for something bigger than herself.

And even though she didn't know it, she was searching for you.

She was searching for your love.

(M.E.K.)

Take Me Home

His arms felt like home,
a place I hadn't visited in months.

(I.D.L.)

Intimidation

His intelligence intimidated her,
stealing away her magical ability with words.

(M.E.K.)

Weeds

Like a weed,
you invaded and took over my entire being.
To them, you were uncontrollably reckless.
To me, you were the most decadent flower I'd ever tasted.

(A.M.N.)

Photographs

He was a dreamer, capturing beauty with the touch of a button.
He found grace where most people did not bother to look.

(G.J.R.)

Capability

He was completely wrong for her in every way.
But in her eyes,
that's what made him perfect.

(D.S.A.)

Always

If I had the choice,
It would be me and you.
You and me.
Us.
Together.
Forever.
Always.

(A.M.N.)

Fun and Games

We were all fun and games.

Until we fell in love.

(I.D.L.)

Conflicted

His ignorance was suffocating,
cheating the room of all its oxygen.
He wrecked everything he ever touched,
leaving no room for beautiful things to grow
within the walls of his sheltered heart.

He was kind and caring,
yet never allowed anyone to see his raw, bare self.
His behavior was destructive,
driving away anyone who ever had the patience to care.
He was scared:
scared of loving, scared of not being loved in return.
But above all, he was conflicted.

He was a confusing mess.

And if he allowed, I would have loved every side of him.

(D.S.A.)

83

Healed Me

You healed me, stitching together all my scattered pieces.
You healed me, only to destruct me in you own distinctive way.

(I.D.L.)

Intruder

He devoured the vicious walls protecting my heart,
barging into a space he was not welcome to enter.
He stormed into my world, consuming what was not his to revel in.

(D.S.A.)

Skyscrapers

He has built his wall up so high
he cannot even see what's on the other side.

(D.S.A.)

Marks

His fingerprints left scripts upon her.

Bruises cover her body,
Marking all the places he ever touched.

(D.S.A.)

Agreement

They cherished one another so much,
they couldn't agree on how to make their love end.

(M.E.K.)

88

Blackout

She drank until he was nothing but a scar of her past.
No amount of poison would be able to undo the tragedy of his love.

(S.P.M.)

89

Monsters

I carry that night around with me,
not as a shackle,
but as a shield
to protect me from monsters like you.

(D.S.A.)

90

Past Mistakes

He wears his past as a faded scar,
giving it enough power to explain him,
but not confine him.
He has changed, leaving behind the mistakes,
struggling to not replicate.

You can see it in his eyes:
The pain, the hurt, and the loss.
Soft wrinkles outline his face, aging him in an unfair manner.
He lived too hard, too fast.
He forfeited too much.
His entire world shifted in a flash.

He's been given a second chance at life,
hoping this time he'll get it right.

(M.E.K.)

Bullets

He played the victim, always blaming others for his wrongdoings.
He wore a bulletproof vest even when he wasn't at war.

(D.S.A.)

Riddle

I've overthought everything I can think of,
still trying to solve the riddle of your love.

(A.M.N.)

93

Selfless Lovers

She loved him so much,
she had to let him go.

(M.E.K.)

Fragile

Our love was too much.
It burned too fast and too bright.

It was scared.
Fragile.

Falling apart with one simple message.

(I.D.L.)

Choices

You chose her,
placing your love upon her left hand.
You chose her,
engraving your toxic love upon me,
caging my heart within its broken ribs.

(S.P.M.)

You

I would have chosen you.
A hundred times:
You.
You.
You.
It always would have been you.
You.

But what about me?

(A.M.N.)

Nightmare

I see you in my nightmares,
haunting from the threads of my own sheets,
lingering in the unoccupied spaces of my mind.

(D.S.A.)

Strong Wind

He was like the wind,
blowing away anything that stood in his way,
taking me with him as he passed by.

He disturbed all the lovely things he ever touched,
destroying anything beautiful in his path.

His tornado of a love devastated me with
just
one
gust.

(T.L.K.)

99

Poisonous Love

She hated herself so much,
wrongly convincing herself she deserved your poisonous love.

(D.S.A.)

Terms of Existence

I hope one day our paths cross again.

Maybe then I'll be wrong for you and you'll be right for me.

Maybe our love can exist under these terms.

(G.J.R.)

Irony

You were everything I desired.
I was everything you never knew you wanted.

Together, we were lighting, striking everything standing in our way.
Together, we were fire, burning down the world that surrounded us.
Together, we were lethal, slowly killing ourselves.

You were everything I never knew I wanted.
I was everything you once desired.

(I.D.L.)

102

Too Much

He made her feel as if she was too much,

When in reality, he was too little.

(D.S.A.)

103

Destiny

She let him go,
not by choice,
by circumstance.

They were doomed from the start.
Nothing.
Nothing would be able to save their love.

(G.J.R.)

Broken Promises

I would say I no longer love you,
but we promised to never lie to each other,

Remember?

(I.D.L.)

105

Departure

I certainly wouldn't have left
if you hadn't pushed me away.

(G.J.R.)

Swimming

I was drowning in the ocean of life.
You were the buoyance keeping me afloat.

Once you left,
I was immensely reminded how much I love to swim.

(M.E.K.)

107

Robbery

One night changed my entire being,
robbing me of everything I use to know.

(D.S.A.)

Promises

He promised to always care for me, to cross oceans for me, literally.
He promised to love me forever, my own personal happy ever after.
He promised me the moon and the stars that dance with it.

He promised me the world.

I wonder what he promised her?

(I.D.L.)

109

Reality

You've forced me to face a reality I'd not ever wanted to know.
A life without you.

A world without us.

(G.J.R.)

Surrender

You hurt me, so I left you.

Touché.

Now our battle can be over.

(I.D.L.)

111

Remorse

He stripped me of everything.

He took everything he wanted,
without a grain of remorse.

(D.S.A.)

Lost Direction

You gave me direction.
You gave me hope.
You were my everything.

What am I suppose to do now that you're gone?

(I.D.L.)

Perspective

If it wasn't for him,
and his pain,
she wouldn't have found her passion.

She could never repay him for almost killing her.

(I.D.L.)

Chaos

He was my favorite type of chaos,
confusingly dragging me into his hazardous world,
revealing the hysteria of my soul.

Still to this day,
he is my favorite type of madness.

(G.J.R.)

Nostalgia

I miss you.

Your void consumes every ounce of me.
Suffocating me from inhaling the air that holds me.
Blinding me from the life, which passes me by.
Compelling me to hold on to your almost-love.

I miss you.

But mostly,
I miss who I was before you ruined me.

(I.D.L.)

Strangers

We will never be the same.

Our love destroyed us,
creating monsters we don't need,
forming strangers we promised we'd never become.

(I.D.L.)

117

Liberation

Finally,
I've been released from the prison of your love.

(M.E.K.)

118

Apologies

Surprisingly, he apologized for not being enough.
He apologized for his mistakes.

Throughout all of this confusion and madness,
she felt sorry he couldn't handle her love.

(I.D.L.)

119

Tears

Every tear shed was his love escaping.
So she sobbed and sobbed until every fiber of his being evaded.

She cried until she no longer carried love for him.

(M.E.K.)

120

Faded

The moment she stopped hating him
was also the same instant her love diminished.
She didn't care enough to hold any hatred.
She felt nothing towards him.

He had become nothing to her.

(I.D.L.)

121

Return

If I ever come running back into your tender arms,
will you promise they will catch me this time?

(A.M.N.)

Every Day

And when they ask how often I think of you,
I'll fake a smile and whisper,

"Every day."

(G.J.R.)

Addiction

Like a drug,
I became addicted to you.
Your touch,
your taste,
your presence,
your substances.
I became addicted to your love.

Once I withdrew myself from your world,
I finally became clean.

(S.P.M.)

Miss Me

"Do you miss me?" he asked.

"It's all I do," she replied.

(A.N.M.)

125

Timing

Timing has never been on my side.

But I'll spend eternity chasing it
for a chance to see you again.

(A.M.N.)

Beautiful Disaster

One day, all this pain and hurt will fade away.
That day, we will be nothing but strangers.
We will solely be two people who use to know one another.
Almost-lovers.
We will be nothing but a piece of each other's past.

And when that day arrives
none of this will have the power to consume us.
None of this will have the power to destroy us.
We will finally be free.
Free from our mistakes and heartbreak,
Free from one another.

Our chapter will be over.
Those pages will hold nothing
but the potential
for how great our love would have been;
how great we would have been.

Those harsh words will tell the tale of you and of me.
A love never given the effort to flourish,
a love never given the chance to become real.

One day,
all this pain and hurt will fade away.
For when that time comes, our story will be over.
Our almost-love will be nothing but a disaster.

Oh, but what a beautiful disaster it will be.

(I.D.L.)

127

Tattoos

The words of our love story will forever be tattooed on me.
They will be engrained within my heart,
appearing as cracks from afar.
I will forever carry around our love.
It defines me.
It has made me into the person I stand as today.
It has made me stronger and wiser.

And mostly,
forgiving.

(G.J.R.)

I'm Sorry

I'm sorry the severity of my love was too much for you all.

(M.E.K., S.P.M., G.J.R., I.D.L., A.M.N., T.L.K., D.S.A.)

Part 4

Recovery

129

Recovery

Leave if you can't fathom staying.
Scream if you want.
Cry if you must.

Then,
pull yourself together,
stand taller than ever,
be greater than before.

Persuasion

She tried and tried to convince everyone to fall in love with her.

Yet all along,
the only person she was trying to convince was herself.

Reconstruction

I rebuilt myself back up from the ashes you left to define me,
never allowing their darkness to dominate the present of my existence.
I rebuild myself back up from the nightmare you place me in,
never allowing the delusion of evil to exhaust.

I rebuilt myself back up from you,
only to find that I thoroughly enjoy
the fire that dances within my daring dreams.

132

Soul Searching

She hadn't quite found her way in this confusing world.
Constantly finding herself within the wrong path.

She searched for a sign,
to help lead her to a state of contentment.
Searching for herself within the darkness of the night sky,
and within the coves of the cold ocean.

She was mesmerizing,
even though her self-esteem conquered
the misled reflection in the mirror.

She knew who she wanted to become,
yet couldn't decide how to get there.

She was beautiful in every sense of the word.

She hadn't quite found her way in this confusing world,
and I loved her for it.

Bleeding

My lips never managed to speak the words my heart has been bleeding to say.

Significant

Her art matters,
her words matter,
her soul matters.

She mattered.

Understanding

Words compiled in her mind,
effortless combing together,
to help make sense of everything she'd never be able to understand.

Scars

Scars outline her entire body, giving her character.
Shaping her into the woman she'd always aspired to be.

Scars outlined her entire body,
telling her story with every mark.

Vanished

She lost herself in
music,
words,
art.

She vanished into anything that held true beauty.

138

Still Silence

The words always came to her late at night
when the world was silent and still.

When nobody else was awake to hear her think.

139

Wildfire

She was like a wildfire,
destroying everything she ever touched.

Home

She never felt at home.

Home had become a feeling to her, not a place.
so she searched and searched for that space,
a sphere of her own,
stumbling across herself in the process of not wanting to be alone.

Changes

She left a little beauty everywhere she traveled,
leaving behind parts of her elegant soul,
and changing the lives of everyone she ever loved.

She believed she could change the world.

And although she never knew it,
somehow,
she did.

Running

Running is easy.
Running is the only thing keeping her moving.
So she ran,
crossing mountains and passing oceans.
She ran until she no longer recognized herself.

She had lost herself in the process of fleeing.
Escaping everything that once tried to hold her down.
Avoiding every demon she'd ever feared.
Running was all she ever knew.

Running is what she has become.

143

Homeless

She no longer had a home
because after a while,
every country,
each person
started to feel like family.

144

Flight

With every country she visited,
she grew,
flourishing into the being she was destined to become.

So she flew and flew,
never allowing her feet to touch the ground
or anything to stand in her way.

She had become greater than anyone ever imagined,
even herself.

145

Freedom

Freedom was what she craved.
So she escaped until freedom was all she owned.

Brutally coming to realize it was far from anything she ever wanted.

146

Wanderer

She was a free spirit,
blowing with the wind.

But all she ever desired
was something to give her a reason to stay.

Friendships

They lift me up every time I fall,
my own personal army,
standing behind me in the wake of war,
battling by my side.

All that I am is a combination of their strengths.

Man on the Moon

She loved the moon.
Not only for the way he shined throughout darkness,
but for how he never completely disappeared.

Changing Seasons

She was like fall,
changing with the colors of the leaves as they descended to the ground,
leaving charm every place she ever fell.

Thunderstorms

She adored the rain,
how it raged wildly and resiliently.

She deeply loved thunderstorms,
for they proved even the heavens lose control sometimes.

Worthy

She saw her own worth.
Yet never understood why they couldn't.

Becoming

I loved her for not only what she was
but what she was about to become.

She reminded me so much of my younger self,
and I would have loved for her to see that.

Dancing Spirit

She had the most exquisite spirit.
It even danced to the silent shatter of heartbreak.

Calming Storms

Her mind was a chaotic mess.
The only way she could calm her storms was to write.

So she wrote
until her demons drowned at sea
and her heart transcribed as the constellations.

Let Go

Let go of all the guilt and remorse.
Let go of your mistakes.

Put down the load you have accumulated;
release this terrible burden you've undeserving created.

True Love

Sometimes
love is breaking our own hearts in hope of bettering theirs.
Setting them free
so another can love them as much as they truly deserve.
Letting them go
so somebody else can love them in a way we'll never.

Sometimes
two people's love is so extraordinary,
they cannot physically survive together.

Their love so strong,
creating unnecessary pressure,
eventually leading to their catastrophe.

Who We Are

Our personalities are embedded in our blood,
pulsing through our entire beings,
permanently in our souls,
forever a part of our existence.

We are who we are.

Vision

Even though our eyes haven't met,
I love the way they look at me.

Love Matters

As life passes by,
all the little things seem insignificant.
We begin to realize all that truly matters is love.

Love from another.

But more importantly,
love from ourselves.

Self-Love

First,
you must love yourself.

Nothing will supercede your own true love.

Single

Single couldn't even begin to describe her.
Strength.
Independence.
Courageous.
Bold.
Fearless.
Spirited.

She was so much more than just one word.

162

Arrival

She got tired of waiting,
anticipating the arrival of a man who may not appear.

So she built up the courage
and became everything she imagined he would be.

163

Delicate Love

I will never settle for a love less delicate
than the love I have found for myself.

Appreciative

Looking back now,
she was grateful for the rejection.

It had led her on a path she never knew.

Through the blindsides,
she ended up in the exact place she'd always wanted to breathe.

Maturity

I've learned the hard way:
you can't control other people.

You can't change them, either.

All you can do is love them for what they are
and forgive them for the rest.

Weaknesses

You are greater than your struggles.
You are stronger than your weaknesses.

167

Forgiveness

Appreciate what has come;
forget everything you've lost.
Move on from things that no longer serve you greatness.

But mostly,
forgive yourself for it all.

Completely Perfect

The more we find ourselves,
the less we need validation from others.
The less we crave the idea of another person making us complete,
we begin to realize we are entirely fulfilled on our own.

We are wholly perfect.

We are perfectly whole.

Peace & Clarity

She let them go,
every single one of them.
She let go of the memories,
the pain,
the empty promises,
the heartbreak.

She finally released everything hurting her heart and soul.
And for the first time in a long time,
she found what she'd really been searching,
peace and clarity.

"The One"

Maybe our greatest love story is falling in love with someone who has been along our sides since the very start.
Maybe our perfect ending involves us putting together the pieces of our own lives,
finally loving ourselves for everything that we are.

Maybe we,
ourselves,
are "the one" we have always been searching for.

171

Life

Life will happen according to its own will.
Sometimes we might not be able to see why today or tomorrow,
maybe not even months from now.
One day it will all make sense.
We will be able to look back and be baffled by where we ended up.

But more importantly,
How we ultimately got there.

Healing

She slowly started to believe in love again.
This is how she knew she had finally healed.

The Sun and the Moon II

The sun and the moon weren't bothered by rejection,
heartbreak,
or departures.
They accepted the fate of the reality of their love.
Never allowing bitterness, jealousy, or hate to exist between them.
The sun burned brighter than ever,
the moon glowed luminously.
Their nevermore destiny remained in grace.
Each morning, the sun will wake and shine her light upon our earth.
Every night, the moon delicately appears through the still darkness.
Their love still the most beautiful to ever exist.

And I believe,
we could all learn from the two of them.

174

This is for all the Girls who Feel Alone

This is for you, my darling girl.
Any girl who feels as if she is alone.
The type of girl who struggles to get through the day.
This one is for the girl who looks so strong, yet feels so weak.
The girl who eventually begins to believe her own fake smile.
This one is for the girl who never gives up.
Who fights like hell, no matter what.
Who picks herself up every time she falls.
To the girl who won't permit to be treated less than she deserves.
This is for any girl who stands for something bigger than herself.
To that girl who screams, "Try me!" instead of whispering "Why me?"
This is for the brave girl who doesn't always feel so daring.
Here's to the girl who smiles throughout the day, yet cries herself to sleep.

The type of girl who doesn't think she's enough.
Pretty enough.
Smart enough.
Good enough.

This is for any girl who has ever felt unwanted and unloved.
For the girl who sometimes feels like she is too much.
The one who cares too much.
Who gives too much of herself to others.
For the girl who tries too hard.
For the girl who understands disappointment too well.
This piece is for the type of girl who loves too much.
Who gives too much of herself to people who clearly don't deserve it.
This is for any girl who has ever gotten her heart completely shattered.

The type of girl who feels too broken to ever be loved again.
This is for the girl who constantly battles with herself,
unnecessarily tearing herself down.
To the girl who lives her life through quotes,
holding on to anything that helps her feel less alone.
This is for any girl who truly does believe she can change the world;
the passionate type of girl.
Any girl who is driven to be better than she ever imagined.
For the girl who doesn't need someone else to take care of her.
That girl who can do it on her own; the independent and strong girl.
This, right here, is for the girl who can't seem to win.
Who has become a close friend to pain and rejection.
Who tries and tries only to get hurt and disheartened in the end.
This is for any girl who feels like she can't catch a break.
Any girl who has ever doubted herself.
Who still questions her abilities.

I'm telling you, this is for every girl who has ever hated herself.
This is for my girl who knows exactly what she wants out of life.
For any girl with big goals and even bigger dreams.
The daydreamers of the world.
This one is for that girl who will never let anything get in her way.
To the girl who says whatever is on her mind.
For every girl who is not afraid to stand up for herself.
I'm writing this for the girl who knows what it feels like to be completely
destroyed by another human being.
For any girl who has ever been dragged down lower than she warrants,
yet can still find love for those who damaged her.

This is for you, my sweet girl.
I wrote this just for you
because you are not alone.

You will never be alone,
for I am one of you.

I wrote this book because you are worth it.
Worth it and so much more.
To remind you, that you are enough.
You are pretty enough.
Smart enough.
Good enough.
You deserve the world.
You deserve everything you have ever wanted out of this life.
I wanted you to know that you are worth being loved.
You are worth the type of love that you have always dreamed of.

Oh dear girl,
I love you.
For you will never be alone.
because I am one of you,
and I always will be.
You are not alone.

You are not alone.

You will never be alone.

About the Author

Kiana Azizian is a born and raised Oregonian. She travels and writes. She's in love with love.

Printed in Great Britain
by Amazon